Leader's Guide

YOUTH FOR CHRIST

Youth Specialties

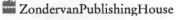

ZondervanPublishingHouse
Grand Rapids, Michigan
A Division of Harper Collins Publishers

Live the Life! Student Evangelism Training Guidebook—Leader's Guide

Copyright © 1998 by Youth for Christ/USA

Youth Specialties Books, 1224 Greenfield Dr., El Cajon, CA 92021, are published by
Zondervan Publishing House, 5300 Patterson Ave. S.E., Grand Rapids, MI 49530.

Written by Todd Temple and Kaylyn Wilson
Edited by Sheri Stanley
Cover and interior design by Razdezignz
See page 39 for a complete list of everyone who helped create the Live the Life! curriculum.

Printed in the United States of America

98 99 00 01 02 03 / / 10 9 8 7 6 5 4 3 2 1

CONTENTS

Welcome!   pg 4
(Optional. If heartfelt welcomes strike you as too sentimental, proceed directly to "How to Use This Curriculum.")

How to Use This Curriculum   pg 5
(Not optional! A must-read overview with only a few details—but boy, are these details ever essential for effectively teaching the lessons!)

Lesson 1	Depend on Jesus	pg 9
Lesson 2	Be Real	pg 15
Lesson 3	Love Others	pg 19
Lesson 4	Share the Gospel	pg 25
Lesson 5	Get Connected	pg 31
Lesson 6	Have Courage	pg 35
Credits		pg 39

WELCOME!

Here are some interesting facts about the Live the Life training project:

The production team worked well over 2,000 hours...
    ...wrote over 40,000 words of scripting
    ...created about 500 multimedia screens using thousands of images
    ...produced nearly 50 video clips
    ...created about 100 pages of text and art for the student guidebook

Are you ready for the most impressive fact? Here it is:
    NONE of what we've created will teach kids to share the gospel.
After all our work, that's a pretty sobering fact. But the truth is, the teaching is out of our hands. Sharing the gospel is a tri-fold relationship between a Christian, a non-Christian, and the God who loves them. So too is evangelism training: a three-part relationship between teacher, students, and the God who seeks to be known. What happens in your training time, between all three parties, won't fit in a video package.

So it's up to you, God, and your students. We trust God to do his part. And we've done all we can to involve students in the learning process. The rest is up to you. We've provided you with hints, tips, and suggested content throughout the course. Get to know this material as well as you can. Become comfortable with it. Let your students see that you are as excited about this course as you hope they will be.

One final thought: when the production team got together to proof the almost-final product, we stopped to pray. Especially, we prayed for you. It felt kind of like we were praying for the parents about to adopt our baby. You don't know it like we do—but in a short time you'll be closer than we ever were.

We've done all that we can do for this child. Now we're giving it to you to raise it, nurture it, and shape it to rock the world. It's not perfect—and we're sure it's got personality quirks that will exasperate and confound you. But we're prayerful, hopeful, and most of all, confident that you'll treat it well. Thanks for your commitment to unleash its message. We hope it changes you and your students as much as it's changed us.

The Live the Life Team

HOW TO USE THIS CURRICULUM

We want you to be effective as you train your students in evangelism. This section explains how the training is put together and what your role is in each element. We can't emphasize preparation enough. The more familiar you are with this training, the easier it will be to make it work perfectly for your students.

We want you to review the entire course before you start, but it is very important to review lessons five and six. These two lessons are based on so many other elements in the program that reviewing them will help you understand the importance of the critical threads that run through the entire course. Instead of introducing new and unrelated ideas, each lesson builds on ideas already presented and keeps building so these ideas become part of long-term memory and regular habits.

That's not to say that each lesson couldn't stand on its own, it could. But, the effectiveness of each lesson is doubled or tripled if students have experienced the lessons that come before it. It's imperative that students commit to the whole training, not just a lesson or two. The value students take from one lesson is nothing compared to the value they take away from the entire training experience.

Each lesson is divided into a series of short segments. Here are the most common segments:

Monologues. You talk, they listen—script provided.
Videos. Teaching happens through video vignettes and our on-screen host, Shannon Lynch.
Talkbacks. Either you or your Student Presenters get feedback from students in the room.
Guidebooks. Students pause for written personal reflection.
Scared Silent. In their Guidebooks students address and ideally conquer their fears in sharing the gospel.
Gutsy Acts. You challenge students to try out what they've just learned.
Life Together. Students process information in small group discussions—one per session.

MONOLOGUES

This is your opportunity to train your students in evangelism. All the other components of the training back up and further explain what you teach during this time. We have written out for you what we recommend you say during the monologue time, but as with everything, we want you to tailor this training to meet the needs of the students in your group.

The VCR is always stopped during your teaching time so there is no reason to hurry (or take forever for that matter). Just keep your group in mind as you prepare what you are going to say and how you are going to say it.

VIDEOS

This is the time when you can sit back and enjoy the teaching taking place on the screen. You will see throughout this Leader's Guide the cues to start and stop the VCR. You will always have an opportunity to set up what is about to happen on the video and also to sum up what just happened on the video.

We recommend that you thoroughly preview all of the video components so you are familiar with each segment as you set it up and reiterate its teaching.

TALKBACKS (OPTIONAL)

It's nice to stop the teaching every once in a while and let the students feel like they're a part of the program. But it's much more than that. Talkbacks don't stop the teaching. They improve on it. Here's why.

Translation please. The strength of a message is often measured by who delivers it. You can say something really spectacular, and students will think, "That's nice." Then one of these same students will stand up and express the same idea, using a personal example, and the rest of the group will think, "That's amazing." Same message, different mouths. Talkbacks give students a chance to express the lesson's most important ideas out of their own mouths.

Taught versus caught. You've played Telephone. That's where you whisper a message in someone's ear, who passes it on to someone else, and so on. Your original message might have been "Mary had a little lamb. Its fleece was white as snow." But when the message is repeated at the end of the line, it comes out, "Larry's lamb went piddle, but the geese didn't have to go." Or something like that.

Well, the same thing happens in teaching. You say one thing, but by the time the message makes it through the air, hair, ears, and distracted brains of the students, it sounds like something totally different. How can you know that students are catching the message—the right message? By fielding comments from the group, you can know what's being caught and what's been dropped—and tailor your message to match.

Give us a break. You may be able to speak for 45 minutes straight, but the ears and rears of your group may not last that long. A Talkback lets the students see and hear and do something else for a few minutes. It changes the pace and pitch, giving students a fresh start for your next batch of words.

Think about it. Let's say you ask a question but have time for just four audience responses. Three people sharing in a room of 25 is not a lot. But there may be a few others who raised their hands to speak, but time prevented your getting to them. And eight more who were thinking about raising their hands but decided not to. Each one of these students already formulated the answer in their heads, because they were ready—or almost ready—to share it. They have interacted with the material far more than if they had merely heard it and moved on.

One quick operations issue related to Talkbacks: If the audience is large enough to prevent everyone from hearing a single person's response from her seat, then it's best to use a microphone and an interview style. If the audience is small enough, it's best to keep students in their seats and let them respond without a mic and an interviewer.

GUIDEBOOKS

Each of your students must have a Guidebook when you begin the training. This is their direct connection to what you are saying and what is being taught on the video. What students choose to write in their Guidebooks will be evidence of what they are getting out of the curriculum.

One section of the Guidebook, Scared Silent, contains a list of fears and hesitations students might have about sharing the gospel with a friend. The extensive list includes just about every fear we can think of that relates to various themes of the training. In Lesson One students are asked to check one of three boxes next to each fear: "It's a fear," "not sure," "no worries." Each subsequent lesson sends students back to the Scared Silent list to cross out any fears that were addressed and conquered in the previous lesson. Ideally, this list will be cut down to almost nothing by the time we arrive at Lesson Six.

The Guidebooks also contain Gutsy Acts (see the next section) where students are challenged to apply what they've learned in each lesson.

Look through the Guidebook and maybe have your own to work through as students go through them, too. It should be obvious by the content of your teaching what pages the students are to be filling out, and occasionally we've given specific page numbers to keep you on track. There are many great insights in the Guidebook that you won't want your group to miss.

GUTSY ACTS

This training course is not about knowing what to do. It's about doing it. Gutsy Acts are critical because they require students to do what they've learned immediately, practically, and measurably. Gutsy Acts give you the opportunity to challenge your students at the end of each lesson to apply what they've just learned. You can ask them to report on their commitment the next time you meet—how they did, what was tough, and whether or not they are willing to carry through on the commitment for an extended period of time.

For each Gutsy Act you can give your students four choices:

The first choice is challenging but attainable.

The second choice adds a new hurdle to the first act; it's a bit tougher.

The third choice is very difficult. Tell your students not to choose it unless they are willing to set aside their own agenda and lay it all on the line for Jesus that day.

The fourth choice is up to them. If none of the first three choices work for them, or they feel like God is calling them to a different act, then have them go with what God is calling them to do.

Students can make different choices for each lesson. They don't have to feel that because they committed to the hardest choice for one lesson, they have to commit to the most difficult for the next lesson. They need to choose each act to match their abilities and guts.

Sharing your faith is not a single bold and scary act. It's the culmination of many smaller, more attainable acts—and each of those preliminary acts remind us of what Jesus can do through us when we allow him the opportunity.

LIFE TOGETHER

These are the small group discussion times to be held at the end of each session. This is a critical time for students to process together all that they have been learning. You need to schedule the Life Together time directly after the training. Save it for a later time only if absolutely necessary.

How you divide up your group is totally up to you—although it's a really good idea to keep the same groups throughout the curriculum. The level of honesty increases as the group continues to meet and share a little bit more each time.

Having your Life Together groups is a continuation of the training. The Life Together group time allows students to process what they are thinking and learning in a safer environment than the large group. A lot of the questions they'll be answering will be similar to those in the Talkback time but with a focus on application. Students who feel uncomfortable answering in front of a group of 25 or more will probably feel more comfortable answering in a group of five or six. It's important to emphasize Life Together groups as part of the training time.

When you schedule time for each lesson, be sure to include at least 10 to 15 minutes for the Life Together small group times.

STUDENT PRESENTERS (OPTIONAL)

As you look through this Leader's Guide, you'll see times when you can have Student Presenters help with the teaching. Students can play a critical part in each lesson. Their ability to interview other students in Talkbacks will make or break these segments. If they do well, you'll hear students sharing things that will shape your own monologues, give you feedback on what's been taught, and add credibility to your words as skeptics hear your message restated in the words of their peers.

As mentioned in the Talkback section, there is a rule of thumb about when to ask your questions in an interview style and when to have students respond from their seats. Make sure your Student Presenters know which format to use for your group.

You'll also see that you have the option of the Student Presenters having a greater role in some of the teaching segments of later lessons. That will take lots of practice on their part, especially since most of their teaching parts are in dialogue with each other or with you. And in the final lesson ("Have Courage") you can have them teach the whole thing. Well, not quite—you can come back to wrap up the lesson and the training course.

Using Student Presenters is a great option for many different reasons:

(1) It challenges your leadership students to get involved and challenge their peers.

(2) It allows you to develop deeper relationships with some of your students.

(3) Research indicates that students are most often influenced by their peers. God may use Student Presenters to reach students that you couldn't reach on your own.

There should be some qualifications for the students you use as presenters. You can make your own list of criteria, but we suggest the following requirements:

• Students who have shared their faith
• Students who are excited about evangelism
• Students who are respected by other members of the group
• Students who can relate to their peers in ways that allow the peers to feel comfortable opening up to them

CONCLUSION

Okay, now you've read all the material, you've reviewed all the training lessons, you're ready to train your students in evangelism. We're excited for you and your group as you embark on this evangelism training adventure. For questions, comments, or feedback, please visit our Web sites at www.livethelife.org or www.YouthSpecialties.com. Share your training experience story with us!

Lesson One
DEPEND ON JESUS

Overview

I must DEPEND ON JESUS instead of relying on myself.

Key Verses Romans 5:8, Ephesians 3:17a

Feelings helpless, rescued, liked

Facts 1. I'm hopeless without Jesus. (He's my SAVIOR.)

2. I need Jesus daily, in every part of my life. (He's my LORD.)

Actions

Now: I will (re)discover what it is that Jesus rescued me from; I will determine which areas of my life I've excluded Jesus from entering and invite him in.

This week: I will spend time with Jesus each day.

Long term: I will spend time with Jesus daily.

In Short

There's no point at all in sharing your faith if you don't have any. This lesson starts at square one: What does it mean to be a Christian? Do I really **DEPEND ON JESUS** in every area of my life? The truth is, if I call myself a Christian, I'm saying that Jesus is my SAVIOR (rescuer from eternal separation from God), and he's my LORD (master of my life and everything in it.) I depend on him eternally and daily.

Background

The Bridge illustration is often used in evangelism as a tool—an impersonal, theological diagram of redemption. This training course **does not** use it this way.

Instead we show students the Bridge illustration and ask them to describe their own rescue story through this picture. The first part of Lesson One invites students to look at their own rescue by Jesus via the Bridge.

Lesson Four, "Share the Gospel," teaches students how to use this personal picture of their own rescue to help another person consider her need for rescue. This method helps students avoid a strictly theological discussion and center their sharing on a heart-to-heart conversation.

In addition to introducing the Bridge illustration, Lesson One sets up many other threads that weave their way through subsequent lessons. Here are a few threaded segments and personalities they'll see for the first time:

• **Scared Silent**. Students will personally examine their own fears and hesitations in sharing the gospel; subsequent checkups help them see how they're conquering their fears.

• **Real Kids**. They'll meet Real Kids via video in this lesson and get to know them throughout the lessons that follow.

• **It's Simple**. They'll meet the Professor and hear his first, beautifully simple explanation; he's got more later.

• **Evangeline**. They'll meet Eva, who has a quirky-cool way of proving that the lesson's message not only relates to evangelism, it's essential to it. She'll rattle skeptics' cages again and again.

• **Gutsy Acts**. Students will commit to their first challenge to act on what they've learned; a new commitment for every lesson.

Outline

A. Training Introduction **[8-10 minutes]**
B. The Point—DEPEND ON JESUS
    1. Intro: What's a Christian? **[5-7 minutes]**
    2. DEPEND ON JESUS as my SAVIOR **[15-18 minutes]**
        Bridge illustration
        Personal rescue story
    3. DEPEND ON JESUS as my LORD **[12-15 minutes]**
        My Heart, Christ's Home illustration
        Quiet time—opening doors
    4. Conclusion **[5-7 minutes]**
        Gutsy Acts
C. Life Together small groups

A. Training Introduction

Begin by welcoming your group and introducing yourself. You may want to share something about yourself if you have new students in your group. Then introduce your Student Presenters and explain how they will be helping throughout the training.

To begin Lesson One, pull out your Bible and read 2 Corinthians 3:18.

"There's no magic formula for sharing your faith. There's no book, tape, tract, T-shirt, song, or verse that will let our friends see Jesus, if they don't first see his reflection in our lives. Let's take off the masks, the costumes—the junk that blocks that cool view."

Lead students in prayer asking the Holy Spirit to "work within us" today, to help us look more and more like Jesus.

"I know why I've invested in this training—to help you understand how to share Christ with your friends. But what about you? Why are you investing in this training?"

STUDENT PRESENTER:
"These could be some reasons—

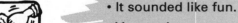

- It sounded like fun.
- You can't ever get up the courage to tell friends about Jesus.
- You had the hots for someone else that was coming.

Turn to page 6 in your Guidebook and answer this question honestly: Why did you come?"

SCARED SILENT

Give some quick illustrations of your own fears in sharing the gospel, then acknowledge that this room is likely filled with unspoken fears.

"I'll bet you have some hesitations, too. Turn to Scared Silent (pages 10-11) in your Guidebook and take an honest inventory of your fears and concerns. You have about 2 minutes."

Allow students two minutes to take inventory of their fears in their Guidebooks, rating their degree of fear in each of dozens of areas.

"Whatever your fears about sharing your faith, I'm asking you to make a choice to dive in 100 percent. Let's spend a moment silently talking to God. Ask him to help you apply everything we'll talk about to your life. Ask him to give you a passion to see your friends come to know Jesus."

"We're going to be spending a lot of time together, and we want to get as much good stuff out of every moment as we can. So we've come up with a few simple rules to max out our time:

- **Show up.** Be in this room, on time, each session, with Bible, Guidebook, and pen.
- **Team up.** Participate in small groups and Talkbacks.
- **Fess up.** Forget about the "Sunday School" answers; be real or be silent.
- **Give up.** Surrender to God—ask him to show you what you need to learn; he wants to tell you!
- **And throw up**—oops, just kidding.

Can we live by these rules? Okay. Now that we've got all the business out of the way, let's begin the training!"

B. The Point—DEPEND ON JESUS

1. INTRO: WHAT'S A CHRISTIAN?

START VIDEO [a little over 2 1/2 minutes]
Shannon Lynch introduces herself as our video host and gives an overview of the six lessons in this training.

Then the video goes right into "What's a Christian?"—word-on-the-street sound bites from kids defining the term. Most definitions sound pretty good except that **all** are about what **we** do—not about what Jesus has done for us.

Shannon comes back to tell us that, "Before we can share our faith, we need to explore what it means to be a Christian."
STOP VIDEO

"So I'm asking you the same question we asked the students on that last video. Turn to page 12 and see if you can write a short definition of what a Christian is."

Allow students a couple of minutes to write their definitions.

2. DEPEND ON JESUS AS MY SAVIOR

START VIDEO [about 6 minutes]
Students are introduced to The Professor in "It's Simple, Part 1: Myth Busters"—it's not what I do that makes me a Christian—it's what Jesus has done **for me**.

Shannon comes on to discuss that we are hopeless without Jesus. Then she introduces how Jesus is our SAVIOR.

Next is "Real Kids, Part 1: I Need Jesus Because..."

Shannon comes back to take us through the Bridge illustration and the five key words—GOD, ME, SIN, JESUS, and TRUST. The video cuts from Shannon to the Bridge illustration which takes students through their own rescue story. Shannon ends by asking, "What stood between you and God? What danger lay in the gap? Different people have different reasons."
STOP VIDEO

"As you saw in the last video, the Bridge illustration contains five key words, and each of the key words has an audio sound associated with it. We'll be using the Bridge illustration many times throughout this training, so every time you hear the sound of one of the key words on the video, yell it out!

Let's go back to Shannon's last questions—'What was your reason for calling out to Jesus for rescue? What stood between you and God? What did Jesus rescue you from?'

Put your answers in the box on the bottom of page 14 in your Guidebook."

Allow students time to work through their Guidebooks.

START VIDEO [1 1/2 minutes plus]
This segment begins with a clip from the movie, *The Crossing*. Then Shannon uses another version of the Bridge illustration.
STOP VIDEO

"How many of you became Christians when you were really young, or didn't quite know everything you were getting yourself into—or out of?
 Well, then for all of you—here's good news! It doesn't matter! Because you've been rescued, whether you knew it or not! It may not seem spectacular when you tell someone how you were saved, but when you consider what you were saved from—well, that's pretty spectacular!"

STUDENT PRESENTER:
Ask students to share their own rescue stories.

3. DEPEND ON JESUS AS MY LORD

START VIDEO [2 1/2 minutes]
This segment begins with "Real Kids, Part 2: Rescued in the Dark" where kids talk about the reality of their rescue.
 Shannon then presents how Jesus is my LORD. A *Lord* is someone you depend on. Do you depend on your LORD?
 Next is "Real Kids, Part 3: My Lord, Right Here, Right Now."
STOP VIDEO

"Take the It Depends survey on page 16. Be honest. In which areas of your life do you **DEPEND ON JESUS** as LORD—and how much do you depend on him in these areas? You have five minutes."

Give students time to complete the survey.

STUDENT PRESENTER:
Ask students to respond to the question, "How do you **DEPEND ON JESUS**?" Have students answer the same questions used in the video.

START VIDEO [a little more than 4 minutes]
As this segment begins, Shannon is making the point of looking to Jesus daily for guidance when she is interrupted by Evangeline. Evangeline explains why **DEPENDING ON JESUS** as LORD has everything to do with evangelism.
 This is followed by "Real Kids, Part 4: Caught in the Act."
 Then Shannon comes on and introduces the booklet, My Heart Christ's Home, by Robert Boyd Munger, which is followed by the segment called "My House."
 Finally, Shannon guides us through the doors in our hearts and explains that, "Jesus wants to live there and show us how to live life to the full with him."
STOP VIDEO

Read Ephesians 3:17.

"Take a moment to wander through your own heart. On page 17 of your Guidebook, you'll see a floor plan of your heart. In each room make a sign by circling the symbol that Jesus sees when he stands outside this door or area of your life: WELCOME, PLEAES KNOCK, or KEEP OUT. When you're done, read the words at the bottom of the page as your prayer to Jesus."

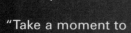

Allow students some time to work through their Guidebooks.

"It can be pretty scary letting Jesus into all the rooms of your life. And just like the door into a hotel room, if you don't stand there and hold it open, it shuts on its own! Sin blows our doors closed daily. That's why it's so important to open those doors daily, to invite Jesus inside, to spend time with him—to seek his guidance—to let him be LORD of each day. That's what a daily quiet time is for. Think of it as a big doorstop, propping open the doors inside your heart so that Jesus is welcome to roam freely."

4. CONCLUSION

START VIDEO [2 minutes exactly]
This segment beings with a clip called "Quiet Time," then Shannon wraps up the lesson.
"**DEPENDING ON JESUS** yourself is the first step to showing others that they need Jesus, too."
STOP VIDEO

"What about you? Are you willing to commit to daily quiet time with Jesus—to open the doors and depend on him as LORD of your life each day?

In each of the lessons of this training, I am going to challenge you to a Gutsy Act: A challenge to act on what you've learned. First turn to page 8 and read the information describing your options for Gutsy Acts. Then turn to page 20 to choose and sign your first commitment. You have two minutes."

Give students two minutes to decide on their Gutsy Acts.

"I dare you to fulfill your Gutsy Act today—and every day throughout this training. If you do it, you'll get a daily reminder that: you **DEPEND ON JESUS** as **SAVIOR**—he rescued you; and as **LORD**—he's your loving master, who wants to spend the day with you, guide you, help you, and protect you.

The next time we meet, we'll see how well you were able to fulfill your commitment. We'll talk about how it felt to do this Gusty Act and what you had to overcome to fulfill it."

C. Life Together small groups

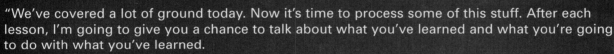

Note: If you didn't divide your group into Life Together small groups before you began the training, you can do it now.

"We've covered a lot of ground today. Now it's time to process some of this stuff. After each lesson, I'm going to give you a chance to talk about what you've learned and what you're going to do with what you've learned.

There are two rules for you to follow in your Life Together small groups. **First rule:** Be honest or be silent. In other words, be real with each other. If you can't be real and tell your group members what's really going on inside, then just say "pass." **Second rule:** Don't blab outside the group. What you say in your Life Together small group is confidential—don't share it beyond the group members. Sound simple? Then go get started. You'll find the discussion questions for this lesson on page 21 in your Guidebook. You have about ___ minutes." *(Give them the amount of time you have or you think they'll need.)*

Close in prayer.

Lesson Two
BE REAL

I must BE REAL in my relationships with others.

Key Verses   Philippians 2:5-7, Ephesians 5:8-11

Feelings   safe, open

Facts
1. To BE REAL, I must humble myself. (GET HUMBLE.)
2. To BE REAL, I must start peeling back the "layers of pretense" in front of others. (GET OUT.)
3. To stay real, I must continue to be honest about who I am. (STAY OUT.)

Actions

Now: I will confess my "charade of perfection" before God (e.g., pride) and identify the hidden issues that keep me from BEING REAL with others.

This week: I will peel off a layer before another person each day this week and be honest about who I am each day.

Long term: I will peel off my layers of pretense in front of a friend outside of this training to let this friend know who I really am.

In Short
The first step to sharing your faith is to DEPEND ON JESUS. The second step is to confess that fact to **others**—to BE REAL. Before you tell others that they need Jesus, you must be willing to reveal how much you need him. This lesson will help you come out of hiding with your faith by showing others who you really are.

Background
DEPENDING ON JESUS includes the acknowledgment to him that we need a Lord—someone to work in and through us to make us in his image. In a sense, when we invite him in as Master of our "house," we are BEING REAL to him—"I'm not perfect, I can't do this on my own, I need you." BEING REAL to our friends means revealing this fact to them, too.

Philippians 2:5-7 is used to contrast Jesus' humbling himself with our own tendency to inflate ourselves. Jesus is perfect, yet he takes on human form. We're **not** perfect, yet we often take on God-like form in our charade of sinlessness. First we must deflate ourselves before God and acknowledge our sinfulness—confess our independence and pride and pretense.

Perfection is defined not as "without flaw," but as "complete, independent, unneedful of God's perfecting work in our lives." With or without awareness of our own flaws, if we pretend that we don't need Jesus, we're prideful and arrogant toward him and need to confess.

Ephesians 5:8-11 talks about the process of bringing the dark, hidden truth about ourselves into the light. In this lesson we call this process *peeling*, or GETTING OUT. The third major point of this lesson also stems from this verse. In it, we call students to a life of STAYING OUT—maintaining the bare-skinned life that we attain when we've peeled back all the layers of pretense.

Outline

A. Review **[6-8 minutes]**
    Flashback
    Scared Silent
B. The Point—**BE REAL**
    1. Intro: The Problems with Pretending **[6-8 minutes]**
    2. GET HUMBLE **[8-10 minutes]**
        Jesus became real to us (Philippians)
        Humility prayer
    3. GET OUT **[8-10 minutes]**
        Peeling layers, dark to light (Ephesians)
    4. STAY OUT **[4-6 minutes]**
        (Ephesians)
    5. Conclusion **[5-7 minutes]**
        Gutsy Acts
C. Life Together small groups

A. Review

"Welcome back. Are you guys excited about starting Lesson Two? Well, before we can start the next lesson, let's look back at the lesson before. There's a lot to remember from Lesson One, so let's try to sum up the most important ideas."

STUDENT PRESENTER:

"What stuck with you? What was the most important thing you heard in the last lesson?"

Allow students some time to answer. Then ask:

"How did you do with the commitment you made in your Gutsy Act from the last time we met?"

SCARED SILENT

"What about our fears? Let's look back over the list on pages 10-11 and see if we've addressed any of your fears and concerns so far. If you've eliminated a fear, cross it out. Not all fears are magically eliminated by the facts. Sometimes it takes weeks, months, or years to overcome them. But it's helpful to mark off the fears that no longer haunt us, so we can work on the ones that still do. That's what this exercise is all about. We'll check these pages again before each lesson."

B. The Point—BE REAL

1. INTRO: THE PROBLEMS WITH PRETENDING

START VIDEO [between 3 1/2 and 4 minutes]
Shannon Lynch gives an overview of Lesson One and what it means to **DEPEND ON JESUS**.
   Then she introduces us to "Found Out, Part 1: So You Want to Be a Christian." This is the first episode in a series of adventures of Brad, a teenager who's discovering that genuine faith is "found out" by his friends through his honesty and weakness, instead of his pretense and strengths.
   Shannon ends with, "When you see people like Brad, I'm sure you say, 'Wow, he is a real Christian!' Right? No?! Why not? What's wrong with acting like Brad?"
STOP VIDEO

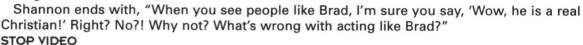

"So what do you think? What is wrong with acting like Brad?"

STUDENT PRESENTER:

Field responses from students then ask:

"Why do we sometimes act like Brad?"

2. GET HUMBLE

START VIDEO [almost 6 minutes]
This segment begins with The Professor in "It's Simple, Part 2: Best Foot Forward"—being a Christian means I show who I truly am, struggles and all.
   Shannon comes on to reiterate that point, then we see "Real Kids, Part 5: The Real Me."
   This is followed by Evangeline who comes in to really make the point for us.
   Then Shannon begins to explain **how** to BE REAL: GET HUMBLE, GET OUT, and STAY OUT. She narrates another version of the Bridge showing how Jesus really became human.
STOP VIDEO

Read Philippians 2:5-7.

"Jesus is God. He's perfect, yet he leaves that awesome place called Heaven and gets right down on earth. That's humility! On the other hand, we're **not** perfect, we're **not** sinless—that's why we need a SAVIOR!"

At this point you can draw a two-column chart up on a board, like this:

JESUS	YOU & ME
PERFECT	IMPERFECT
SINLESS	SINFUL
HUMBLE	NEED A SAVIOR

"And to play a charade, to **pretend** that we **don't** need Jesus, to act as though we're above it all, or at least to pretend that our sins are **too big** for him to handle, or **too small** to bother him—that's like a slap in Jesus' face. We need to stop this offensive charade. Before we GET OUT of hiding and show others who we really are, we need to GET HUMBLE before Jesus—to admit that we're **not** perfect or complete or independent. And we must ask Jesus to forgive us for sometimes pretending that we are.

   Let's take this step now. Turn to page 25 in your Guidebook and read the prayer silently as your prayer to Jesus. You have about a minute."

3. GET OUT

START VIDEO [4 1/2 minutes plus]
Shannon introduces the second step toward BEING REAL: GET OUT.
   Then comes "Found Out, Part 2: So You Want to Be a Christian, The Sequel."
STOP VIDEO

"Just like Brad's friends, your friends won't see the real Jesus alive in you if they can't see who you really are! You've got to GET OUT from behind all those layers—the fear, the pretended perfection, the covered-up sins—and let people see who you really are, struggles and all.
   Our friend Paul talks about this process—it's a matter of GETTING OUT of the darkness and stepping into the light."

Read Ephesians 5:8-9.

"The problem is, most of us have so many layers of darkness hiding the real us, that GETTING OUT from behind them all takes really hard work. The solution? Peel off one layer of darkness at a time.
   Are you ready to take the second step to BEING REAL with others? Then prepare to GET OUT of the darkness, one layer at a time. Let's consider one of those layers right now. What's a secret

sin, fear, or imperfection you've been hiding from others? Take the challenge on page 27 in your Guidebook."

Allow students time to answer the questions in their Guidebooks.

4. STAY OUT

START VIDEO [exactly 1 minute]
Shannon shows us the third step in this process, STAY OUT. "GETTING OUT of the darkness is tough, but STAYING OUT is tougher."
STOP VIDEO

"Then how do we STAY OUT of that darkness? Paul's got some 'darkness repellent' for us. Let's pick up where we left off—"

Read Ephesians 5:10-11.

"Tough words! Rebuke. Expose. How? Here are a few STAY OUT tips:
   First, get friends who STAY OUT, too. You know how when you're with certain friends, you're more tempted to play in the dark. But with friends who are committed to STAYING OUT with you, you tend to play in the light. You become a positive influence on each other.
   Second, invite them to tell you what you need to hear. In other words, give them permission to be totally honest with you when they think you're messing up. Your parents showed this kind of loving concern for you when you were a kid: 'Watch out for that truck,' 'If you eat all that candy you'll get sick,' 'Go to the bathroom now before you wet your pants'—stuff like that. Now it's time to let your friends warn you about your behavior. Real love looks like that.
   Third, be accountable to them. Don't wait for them to catch you messing up. Have the guts to reveal your struggles before you go off the deep end.
   Fourth, confess to them your bouts with darkness. Tell them when you've messed up. You need their support and prayer.
   Finally, keep short accounts with Jesus. Don't pile on a list of sins and failures—go to God whenever you mess up, whenever you catch yourself slipping back into the darkness.
I'm not saying any of these things are easy. But I do know this: People in this dark world are searching for hope, for truth, for light. That light comes from Jesus. STAY OUT in the light and people will find Jesus in you!"

5. CONCLUSION

START VIDEO [just shy of 2 minutes]
The first segment here is "Real Kids, Part 6: Staying Out is No Picnic."
   Shannon sums up the three steps to BEING REAL: GET HUMBLE, GET OUT, and STAY OUT. "When others see how much you need Jesus, they'll discover they need Jesus, too."
STOP VIDEO

"Time for another Gutsy Act—a challenge to live today what you've learned today. Turn to page 32 in your Guidebook for this lesson's challenge."

Allow students about a minute to write in their Guidebooks.

C. Life Together small groups

"Last thing, get into your Life Together groups and go through the questions on page 33. Remember the rules: Be honest or be silent, and don't blab outside the group."

Close in prayer.

Lesson Three
LOVE OTHERS

I must **LOVE OTHERS** *so that they will see Jesus alive in me.*

Key Verse   Luke 10:27b

Feelings   obedient, useful

Facts   Intro: Jesus commands me to love my neighbor as myself.

1. Who's my neighbor? *Everyone.*
2. Why love them? *It's how Jesus reveals himself to others.*
3. How do I love myself? *By doing what's best for me.*
4. How will I **LOVE OTHERS**? *By doing what's best for them.*

Actions

Now: I will document examples of my own self-love in action, identify some of the long-term needs of three of my friends, and commit to a specific act of service to help them satisfy these needs.

This week: Each day this week, I will make a specific act of love in the interest of another.

Long term: I will carry out my acts of service for my friends.

In Short

Okay, so you **DEPEND ON JESUS**, and you're **BEING REAL** so your friends know you do. Now it's time to tell them about Jesus, right? Not quite. If you're a disciple of your Lord Jesus, you'll do what he says. And what he says is, **LOVE OTHERS**. This lesson shows you how to **live** the gospel, before you tell the gospel.

Background

The underlying question is, Why did Jesus command us to **LOVE OTHERS**? One of the reasons is that Jesus doesn't show himself bodily to folks these days. The only way for people to see Jesus is to see evidence of him in us. If he's the invisible wind, we're the tree branches that sway as a result. Others can't see the wind—they can only see us moving because of it. Jesus commands us to **LOVE OTHERS** because he knows that's the only way people will see him.

Next question: Why does he tell us to "Love your neighbor as yourself"? Surely he knows that many of us have little love for our own miserable selves. Why didn't he give us a better model of love by saying, "Love your neighbor like God loves you?" Maybe he's giving us an easier target to shoot for. Maybe he's giving us a sliding scale: If we love ourselves very little, we're incapable of showing great love for others, so he asks us to love our neighbor at least that much. And as we act lovingly toward others, we sense our purpose in Jesus and his love for us—and that increases our self-love, which increases our love for others, and so on. He set the standard just above our heads—and it stays just within our reach, no matter how tall we grow.

Of course, we need to know how we love ourselves. It's like this: We believe that we're worth more than our actions; that we do bad things, but that we're better than (i.e., worth more than) what we do. And every time we do what's best for our health, education, reputation, soul, and future, we prove our self-love. Jesus asks us to act in these same ways—not in self-interest, but in the interest of others. That's exactly how he treats us—and how he reveals himself to others through us.

Outline

A. Review **[5-7 minutes]**
     Flashback
     Scared Silent
B. The Point—LOVE OTHERS
     1. Intro: Jesus' commandment (Luke)
     2. Who's My Neighbor? **[7-9 minutes]**
     3. Why Love Them? **[13-15 minutes]**
     4. How Do I Love Myself? **[13-15 minutes]**
     5. How Do I LOVE OTHERS? **[6-8 minutes]**
     6. Conclusion **[4-6 minutes]**
          Gutsy Acts
C. Life Together small groups

A. Review

Introduction, welcome back, etc. Open in prayer.

STUDENT PRESENTER:

"As you look back at our last session, what stood out as being most important to you? What hit you the hardest? What's the most important thing you heard? What is the most important part of BEING REAL?"

After students have answered these questions, ask:

"Did anything happen to you as a result of what you learned or did in your Gutsy Act?"

SCARED SILENT

Affirm answers, then say:

"Let's return to the Scared Silent survey to see if we've addressed any of your fears and apprehensions so far. If you've eliminated a fear, cross it out."

B. The Point—LOVE OTHERS

1. INTRO: JESUS' COMMANDMENT (LUKE)
2. WHO'S MY NEIGHBOR?

START VIDEO [a little over 3 1/2 minutes]
Shannon reviews Lessons One and Two, then introduces the next lesson, LOVE OTHERS.
   Next we hear from The Professor in "It's Simple, Part 3: Remember Two Things."
   Then Shannon introduces us to four key questions and begins with question one, Who's My Neighbor? "In fact, someone asked Jesus that very same question. He answered with a famous story."
STOP VIDEO

STUDENT PRESENTER:

"Anyone have a clue of the name people have given Jesus' famous story?" (Good Samaritan)

Ask a series of questions about the story, allowing the group to make the points.

"Summarize the story for us. Why did he choose a Samaritan as the hero? Based on the story, which kinds of people are what Jesus calls *neighbors*?"

"The story of the Good Samaritan is pretty popular. You've probably heard it or read it dozens of times. Unfortunately that makes it easy to miss the point. Remember, Jesus used the story to define what he meant when he said *neighbor*. He chose that word carefully. Think about it: Jesus could have said, 'Love your brother,' or 'Love your best friend,' or 'Love people who think and look and talk and act and believe like you.'

But that's not what he said. He said *neighbor* and then defined the term to include even our enemies and those we despise! In other words, he wants us to love everybody! So according to Jesus, who is my neighbor? Everyone in my world! That's a big neighborhood! Ever stop to think about the number of people you see in your world every day? It's a **big** world."

3. WHY LOVE THEM?

START VIDEO [3 1/2 minutes]
This segment begins with "Nadia's World."

Then Shannon shares that since we now know **who** Jesus wants us to love, let's go on to the question, Why love them? She is interrupted by Evangeline who explains why we should love them. Shannon concludes, "Jesus reveals himself to other people through our love."
STOP VIDEO

To make the next point, play a game called "What Is That?" There are different ways to set this game up. You can go all out or do it on a much smaller scale. Read through the explanation and decide what will work best for your group. To make this really big, put on a goofy polyester jacket, sport coat, or tux jacket—the wilder, the better. Also, keep the game moving very quickly. Talk fast, move fast, don't expand on ideas here. You may want to make a large sign that says WHAT IS THAT? and have a student hold it up at all the appropriate times.

In this game, contestants try to guess the object being demonstrated by the celebrity guest. The catch is the contestants can't see the object—they can only see the celebrity acting it out!

Choose three students from the crowd and bring them up front. Introduce them to the group and then go out and pick your celebrity guest. Play this up!

"Well,_____, we're honored to have you here. In just a moment, I'm going to show you an object. The contestants won't see it. Your job is to act out this object while the contestants try to guess what it is. You can't say a word—they must guess it only by your actions."

Take the three contestants out of the room and present the object to your celebrity guest. Use something like a toilet brush or a plunger. Then bring in your contestants and have the celebrity begin acting it out. Let the contestants guess for a while.

After the contestants have guessed, hold up the object for them to see; congratulate the winner if there is one; thank all students for playing; etc. Then remove jacket and game-show host demeanor.

"What was the point of all this foolishness? That's a lot like what happens when we LOVE OTHERS. We can't show people Jesus himself. We can't even show them a photograph. We can only act him out—show others what Jesus does. What does Jesus do? **He loves others!**"

4. HOW DO I LOVE MYSELF?

START VIDEO [2 minutes and 40 seconds]
Shannon introduces "Found Out, Part 3: Caught in the Act." Brad tries to help someone in need, but the recipient of his kindness misinterprets his motives.

Then Shannon introduces the third question, "How do I love myself? By doing what's best for me."
STOP VIDEO

This next skit will help illustrate the point of loving myself by doing what's best for me. You will probably want to write some of these answers on a board or an overhead. Read this through thoroughly and decide how you want to present this illustration.

Bring one of your Student Presenters up front and begin this dialogue:

Youth Leader:	Can I ask you a personal question? When you got up this morning, you made an important choice about . . . brushing your teeth. I want to know the choice you made this morning. Was it BRUSH or DON'T BRUSH? What was it?
Student Presenter 1:	I chose to BRUSH.
Youth Leader:	Good for you! And great for all the people you talk to today! Let's look at the top three reasons people choose to brush their teeth. *(Show your answers on a board or overhead.)* KEEP TEETH AND GUMS HEALTHY . . . COMBAT BAD BREATH . . . and TO AVOID THE DENTIST. _____, which of these three reasons is most important to you?
Student Presenter 1:	I don't know, they're all important. I guess the first one.
Youth Leader:	*(Reveal a second side of the answer—either next to it on the overhead or on the board. The answer should read WHAT'S BEST FOR ME!)* So your teeth won't fall out, so you won't walk around toothless. Basically, because you've decided that brushing your teeth is what's best for you!
Student Presenter 1:	*(enthusiastically)* Right!
Youth Leader:	Okay, let's check out the other reasons . . . combat bad breath. *(Reveal the other side to the answer: WHAT'S BEST FOR ME!)* So people will stand near you, so you won't kill people, because your social life is important. In other words, it's still what's best for you! What about the third option . . . avoiding the dentist. *(Reveal the other side to the answer: WHAT'S BEST FOR ME!)* The pain, the Novocain, that sucking thing they put in your mouth, the drill. You've decided that going to the dentist is no fun. Brushing your teeth helps to shorten those dreaded visits to the dentist . . . it's what's best for you. This game is rigged! No matter which reason you have for brushing your teeth, you choose to do it because it's best for you! Okay, what about the other option: DON'T BRUSH. Which brings me to _____. *(Pick another Student Presenter.)*
Student Presenter 2:	Thanks a lot! I brushed my teeth!
Youth Leader:	Do you brush them every morning?
Student Presenter 2:	Usually.
Youth Leader:	Sometimes you don't.
Student Presenter 2:	Occasionally.
Youth Leader:	I'm calling your mom—later. Right now we're on to something else. Here are the three stupidest reasons people DON'T BRUSH. *(Show your answers on a board or overhead.)* USED TOOTHBRUSH TO CLEAN THE TOILET . . . TOO MUCH WORK . . . and STILL ENJOYING THAT PIZZA FROM LAST NIGHT. What is it _____ ? Choose one of your reasons.
Student Presenter 2:	Well, it takes a lot of effort to brush all these teeth—I choose number two.
Youth Leader:	Why? Too much work, gotta conserve energy for tying shoes, resting is more important than clean teeth to you . . . *(Reveal the other side to the answer: WHAT'S BEST FOR ME!)* In other words, you've chosen what you think is best for you. I'll buy you an electric toothbrush. Well, let's check the other reasons. What about that toilet cleaning thing . . . *(Reveal the other side to the answer: WHAT'S BEST FOR ME)* Too disgusting, might make you sick, then you'd have to brush all over again. NOT brushing is best for you in this case, too. How about that last reason? Savoring the taste of last night's pizza . . . *(Reveal the other side to the answer: WHAT'S BEST FOR ME!)* Hey, it was good pizza. Why ruin a good thing? Maybe you won't need breakfast now. Yep, in this case, you've decided that NOT BRUSHING is what's best for you at that moment. Even when we make decisions that aren't healthy, we choose them because we think that they're best for us at that moment.

5. HOW DO I LOVE OTHERS?

START VIDEO [4 minutes plus]
Shannon further explains how we make decisions based on what's best for me at that moment.
She then explores the concept of perspective when it comes to loving ourselves.
   Next we hear from The Professor in "It's Simple, Part 4: Love Thy Neighbor."
   Shannon then helps us understand the fourth question, How do I **Love Others**?
STOP VIDEO

"This is why Jesus tells us to do the seemingly impossible things like love our enemies and pray for those who hurt us. He's got an **eternal** perspective; he's looking at the ultimate goal. He's counting on you to point people to **him**!
   Let's see how Jesus' eternal perspective can change the way you treat others."

STUDENT PRESENTER:

"Give us a teaching of Jesus—something Jesus said about how we should treat others—then be honest and describe how you need to apply this perspective toward someone in your own life."

Example: Jesus says that we are supposed to forgive others. Last week I had an argument with a friend about_____. I ignored her all week because I was mad at her. I need to call her and say I'm sorry.
Hint: A list of verses appears on page 41 in the Guidebook.

6. CONCLUSION

START VIDEO [almost 1 1/2 minutes]
First the Bridge illustration, then Shannon wraps up. "Our **love** is **evidence** of **Jesus**!"
STOP VIDEO

"A few minutes ago we took a walk through Nadia's world, seeing people through her own eyes. We saw her classmates, friends, teachers, and family—a total of 448 people in her world in just one day.
   Now, I want you to turn to page 41 and wander through your own world to identify a few key people you know who don't know Jesus. Write down their names. For each of these people, see if you can come up with three specific actions you can take to love them from Jesus' perspective. That is, to do what's best for them eternally. You have about three minutes."

Allow students time to work through names and actions.

"Okay, now that you've done that, turn to page 44 and take one more step in this challenge to **Love Others**. Commit to today's Gutsy Act."

Give students time to choose their Gutsy Act.

C. Life Together small groups

"Again, we covered a lot of material today. Let's take some time in our Life Together groups to process all of this information. Get in your groups and spend some time going through the questions at the end of this lesson. Feel free to share your commitments with each other and be sure to hold one another accountable to the things you say you will do."

Close in prayer.

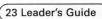

Lesson Four
Share the Gospel

I must Share the Gospel so that others understand that it's good news for them.

Key Verses Romans 5:8, 1 Corinthians 3:7-8

Feelings thankful, enthusiastic

Facts
1. The Good News is good news for **me**!
2. Is it good news for **you**?

Actions

Now: I will tell the Good News story to another person; I will document and tell my own good news story to another person.

This week: I will commit to Share the Gospel with a friend.

Long term: I will Share the Gospel with a friend.

In Short

If you truly Depend on Jesus, and others know that fact (you're Being Real), and you're Loving Others like Jesus says, then you're ready to open your mouth and tell them the Good News. This lesson shows you how.

Background

In Lesson One we showed students the two essential roles of Jesus in our lives: First, he's our Savior—he has rescued us from eternal separation from God by becoming a Bridge between our imperfect, sinful selves and a perfect, sinless God. We used the Bridge illustration to convey the nature of this spiritual rescue. In Lesson Four, we teach students how to use the Bridge illustration to explain this rescue to others. What Jesus did, he did for everyone. The Good News is indeed good news for all.

While the rescue is universally available, each of us perceives the rescue in different ways. Some of us sense a need to be rescued from hell, others call for help when they discover that they're trapped in destructive sin; still others are swallowed up in purposelessness and are brought to the edge of the cliff in a search for meaning. Whatever felt need brings us to the edge, Jesus the Savior provides the Bridge to salvation. This individual rescue from a universal plight is what makes Jesus our personal Savior.

As described in the introduction notes to Lesson One, the Bridge is being used not merely as an evangelism tool, but as a personal picture of the student's own rescue. The act of sharing his faith begins by showing this picture to a friend. It's a personal recounting of a very personal story.

The second step to Sharing the Gospel is to invite the friend to look at his own life through this picture. "Where do you stand in the picture? What separates you from God?" This lesson gives students an opportunity to practice this method, and gives suggestions about what to do with the various answers they may get to their questions.

Outline

A. Review [5-7 minutes]
   Flashback
   Scared Silent
B. The Point—SHARE THE GOSPEL
   1. Intro: Good News for Everyone [7-9 minutes]
   2. Good News for **Me** [6-8 minutes]
      My good news story
      My good news picture
      Practice
   3. Good News for **You**? [12-15 minutes]
      Questions
      Answer: no
      Answer: maybe
      Answer: yes
   4. Conclusion [4-6 minutes]
      Gutsy Acts
C. Life Together small groups

A. Review

Welcome group. Open in prayer.

STUDENT PRESENTER:

"Okay, what was the most important thing from the last lesson, LOVE OTHERS? What stuck with you?"

Allow students time to answer, then ask:

"How did your Gusty Acts go? What effect did the fulfillment of your Gutsy Act have on you this time? Did you have any obstacles to overcome?"

SCARED SILENT

"Time to check your Scared Silent survey again. If we helped you eliminate a fear or concern in the last lesson, cross it out."

B. The Point—SHARE THE GOSPEL

1. INTRO: GOOD NEWS FOR EVERYONE

START VIDEO [5 1/2 minutes]
Shannon goes through the previous three lessons and then introduces the fourth, SHARE THE GOSPEL
   Next is The Professor in "It's Simple, Part 5: Good News!", followed by "Real Kids, Part 7: The Good News Is Really Good News."
   Then Shannon comes back to ask us if everyone has a need to meet Jesus—is the Good News good for everyone? "I know some people who make me wonder, do they really need the gospel?"
STOP VIDEO

STUDENT PRESENTER:

"Well, what do you guys think? Does everyone really need Jesus? Why or Why not?"

After students have finished answering, read Romans 5:8.

2. GOOD NEWS FOR ME

START VIDEO [a little over 2 1/2 minutes]
Shannon shows us how everyone needs Jesus with another version of the Bridge illustration. Then Evangeline interrupts and explains how it's all evangelism.

Shannon tells us how to SHARE THE GOSPEL in two steps: (1) Share why it's good news for me and (2) Ask if it's good news for you. Shannon then explains how the good news is their personal rescue story, "It's the story of how Jesus, your SAVIOR, rescued you from trouble."
STOP VIDEO

"Flip back to page 14 in your Guidebook. Remember, Jesus as SAVIOR rescued you from hell, or destructive sin, or purposelessness, or stumbling into any of these things when you weren't even aware of the danger. If you were to write your rescue story in a way that others could understand it, what would you write?

Okay, then write it! Turn to page 48 and summarize your own rescue story as if someone else were to read it. Be sure to include what Jesus rescued you **from**, and what he rescued you **to**. You have about three minutes."

STUDENT PRESENTER:
Ask a few students to read their completed stories.

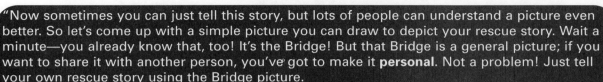

"Now sometimes you can just tell this story, but lots of people can understand a picture even better. So let's come up with a simple picture you can draw to depict your rescue story. Wait a minute—you already know that, too! It's the Bridge! But that Bridge is a general picture; if you want to share it with another person, you've got to make it **personal**. Not a problem! Just tell your own rescue story using the Bridge picture.

In other words, **draw** the Bridge picture, but describe **your own** rescue as you do it. Use the key words, but speak in first person: I, me, my, and so on. Here's how I'd use this picture to tell **my** good news story."

Draw your story up on a board or overhead and be sure to use the key words GOD, ME, SIN, JESUS, and TRUST.

"Here's what I want you to do. On page 49, you've got some space for drawing your rescue picture. I want you to pair off with someone next to you. Take turns drawing your own rescue picture and telling your story to each other."

Allow students time to get through their rescue pictures.

3. GOOD NEWS FOR YOU?

START VIDEO [6 minutes exactly]
Shannon talks about step two in SHARING THE GOSPEL: Ask, "Is it good news for you?"

Next we see "Found Out, Part 4(a): Thanks, But No Thanks." Brad shares his story with a friend then asks him if he would like to choose Jesus as his SAVIOR. The friend says no!
STOP VIDEO

"Sometimes, you tell your story, show the picture, ask good questions, and in the end, the person says no! Is your job over? Same answer! **No.** You keep doing what you've been doing, which is—BE REAL: Continue to show them who you really are, struggles and all. Let them see Jesus alive and at work in you. LOVE OTHERS: Remember, your love is evidence of Jesus. Some people need lots of evidence! And most of all, DEPEND ON JESUS: Continue to pray for your friend and ask Jesus to shine through your love.

Remember, he's still got that eternal perspective. He may give you or someone else another part to play in this person's life. Check it out—"

Read 1 Corinthians 3:7-8.

START VIDEO [1 minute and 13 seconds]
Shannon introduces "Found Out, Part 4(b): Lemme Get Back to You." This time when Brad asks the question, he gets a "maybe" answer.
STOP VIDEO

"When you ask, 'Is this good news for you?' they might say, 'Maybe' or 'I'll think about it' or 'I'll get back to you.' This seed just may take root right away! Here's what you can do to help that happen. First of all, affirm their answer.

Thinking, questioning, considering, searching—these are **good** things! Tell your friend you respect that. Second, ask your friend, 'What keeps you from saying yes?' Maybe you can answer the concern. Maybe you can't. Maybe you can talk to a friend, pastor, youth leader, or someone else who may be able to give you the answer. Then you can follow up by sharing it with your friend. Third, invite your friend to a place where he or she will hear the gospel—church, a youth group activity, concert, or whatever. Maybe when your friend hears the Good News from a different point of view, it will make things clearer. And most importantly, **keep praying!**"

START VIDEO [1 1/2 minutes plus]
Shannon introduces "Found Out, Part 4(c): Good News." In this episode Brad gets a yes.
STOP VIDEO

"Believe it or not, sometimes when you ask, 'Is this good news for you?' the person says **yes**! Now what do you do? This is the exciting part. First, you can lead them in prayer."

Ask two students to volunteer—could be your Student Presenters. Have them go through the following conversation. Make sure you've prepared them before this lesson so they aren't reading it.

STUDENT PRESENTERS:
Student 1: I'm going to talk to Jesus out loud, and you can say the same things to him silently as I'm praying, okay?
Student 2: *(looking a bit awkward)* Okay.
Student 1: Dear Jesus, thanks for rescuing me. I'm sorry for my selfishness, for my sins, for living wrong, for offending you. Please forgive me. Wipe away my sins. I'm trusting you as my Savior. I want to live with you and for you forever. *(then to Student 2)* Do you have anything you want to say to him?
Student 2: Thanks, Jesus, for saving me. I want to live with you, for you. Amen.

"Or something like that. Of course, it's kind of awkward to do this in front of all these people! You want to do this in a private place—just the two of you.

The next point, ask the person to tell someone about his or her decision. Part of being a Christian means **acknowledging** that you are.

Third, you should call your friend the next day and see what's up. Ask your friend what he's thinking, if he's had a chance to pray, if he has more questions. Follow-up is important.

The fourth thing seems obvious, but you can't forget it. You should invite the person to youth group, Bible study, or a church service. You need to get him connected to other Christians as soon as possible so he can start growing in his faith. It can be awkward joining a new group. It's your job to make it smooth.

Finally, **pray!** These first few weeks in a new Christian's life can be pretty tough. Ask Jesus daily to guide this new Christian.

Now that's a lot of stuff to remember, so it's all printed with some other tips in your Guidebook."

4. CONCLUSION

START VIDEO [exactly 1 minute]
Shannon wraps up the lesson on SHARING THE GOSPEL.
STOP VIDEO

STUDENT PRESENTER:

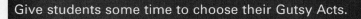

"Let's take some time and hear from some of you who have shared the gospel with a friend. What was it like? What did the person say? What happened afterward?"

"Guess what? Time for Gutsy Acts. Turn to page 54 and choose your act to complete today. Choose carefully."

Give students some time to choose their Gutsy Acts.

"Remember, SHARING THE GOSPEL takes two steps: Tell why it's good news for me and ask, 'Is it good news for you?'"

C. Life Together small groups

"We've covered a lot of ground in this lesson. Let's break into our Life Together groups and talk about what you've learned. The questions are on page 55."

Close in prayer.

Notes

Lesson Five
GET CONNECTED

I must GET CONNECTED so that others can help me, and I can help them.

Key Verse   Galatians 6:2
Feelings   surrounded, unified
Facts   Intro: The need for a team.
1. Form a TEAM OF FOUR.
2. GET A COACH to act as advisor.
3. LIVE THE LIFE TOGETHER: BE REAL, LOVE OTHERS, DEPEND ON JESUS.

Actions

Now: I will identify the players on my team.
This week: I will pray for guidance from God regarding why we're together and how we're supposed to play; I will commit to become accountable to three other team members; I will commit to a mission objective.
Long term: I will carry out these team commitments.

In Short
Up till now, we've been speaking of faith and evangelism at a personal level. Now it's time to look at the big picture. Whether you know it or not, you're just one member of a team of believers, all dependent on Coach God, and all committed to recruiting new members. This lesson shows you how to keep your team in top form.

Background
By the time we reach this lesson, the training has focused on three Christian themes: DEPEND ON JESUS, BE REAL, and LOVE OTHERS. Unbeknownst to the students we have also shaped their small group discussions around these three themes. In each discussion, we've asked students to focus on Jesus in prayer and worship (DEPEND ON JESUS), share honestly from their own hearts (BE REAL), and discuss experiences, goals, and plans in their relationships (LOVE OTHERS).

In this lesson, we reveal this sneaky trick of ours, and show them how "Live the Life" isn't just an individual evangelism strategy—it's a biblical model for living and growing in Christian community.

This strategy will drive home the key themes of the training every time students get together for a team meeting. And as they look back on the small group discussions this week, they'll see that this strategy already works—and works well.

Outline

A. Review [**5-7 minutes**]
      Flashback
      Scared Silent
B. The Point—**GET CONNECTED**
    1. Intro: Christianity—A Team Sport [**6-8 minutes**]
    2. **TEAM OF FOUR** [**5-7 minutes**]
    3. **GET A COACH** [**2-4 minutes**]
    4. **LIVE THE LIFE TOGETHER** [**10-12 minutes**]
        BE REAL
        LOVE OTHERS
        DEPEND ON JESUS
    5. Conclusion [**5-7 minutes**]
        Gutsy Acts
C. Life Together small groups

A. Review

Welcome group. Open in prayer.

STUDENT PRESENTER:

"Let's talk a little bit about what we remember from the last lesson. What stood out to you? What hit you the hardest? What was the most important thing you heard?"

Affirm students' comments, then ask:

"Did anything happen as a result of what you learned or did in your Gutsy Act?"

"Now, let's go back and see if we've identified any other fears or concerns. If you eliminated some of those fears in the last lesson, cross them out. Remember, some of these fears take weeks, months, even years to get over. But we want to continue to eliminate the ones we can so we know which fears to address and work on."

B. The Point—GET CONNECTED

1. INTRO: CHRISTIANITY—A TEAM SPORT

START VIDEO [4 1/2 minutes]
Shannon gives a recap of the last four lessons and then introduces the fifth faith-sharing step: **GET CONNECTED**.
    Next we hear from The Professor in "It's Simple, Part 6: Man of Mystery."
    Finally Shannon explains that to be a Christian is to live in the family of Christ: "Just about

every page in the New Testament talks about the importance of **GETTING CONNECTED** with other members in this family."
STOP VIDEO

Read Galatians 6:2.

"Troubles, problems. Sounds like a pretty normal family to me."

Let students look up and read the following verses about the importance of **GETTING CONNECTED**: John 13: 12-17, Acts 2: 42-47, 1 Corinthians 12: 12-13, Ephesians 2: 19-22, Philippians 4:2-3, and Hebrews 10:25.

"One of the greatest thrills and toughest challenges of the faith is **GETTING CONNECTED** with other Christians. We are a team. We can't play this faith alone. Although, some people try—"

2. TEAM OF FOUR

START VIDEO [just shy of 3 1/2 minutes]
First we see "The Amazing Precision Marching Band."
   Then Shannon shares the three steps to GETTING CONNECTED: Get a TEAM OF FOUR friends, GET A COACH, and LIVE THE LIFE TOGETHER. "First, get four friends. This whole plan starts with a group of friends. It won't work without them."
STOP VIDEO

You may have a different number than four in mind for your teams. You may want to organize these groups a little differently than this training does. That's fine. You can take this section of the training and rewrite what you want to say. We've written it out for you with four, but feel free to change it to a different number or format.

"Four is a good number—big enough to make a team, but small enough to keep it manageable. Who should be on your team? Friends who can be trusted, who share your commitment to Jesus, who can be real, who aren't afraid to hold you accountable, who can commit to weekly time together, and who are of the same gender. Those should be the qualifications for the members on your team.

   Of course, you've got to figure out a weekly time to meet. If your life is like most in this room, you've got a full week with school, sports, jobs, and church activities, etc. You don't need to create another meeting; just set a time—it could be just 20 or 30 minutes long. This could happen before school, at lunch, after school, before Bible study, after church. Whatever works best for the four of you. It's just once a week.

   Here's what I'd like you to do: Take a moment to jot down some names of friends who might meet the qualifications of a team member and who might be willing to set aside a little time each week to get together. You can write these names on page 57 in your Guidebook."

Allow students some time to think of some names and write them in their Guidebooks.

3. GET A COACH

START VIDEO [half a minute]
Shannon introduces the next step in GETTING CONNECTED: GET A COACH. "You can't have a winning team without a coach."
STOP VIDEO

Again, you may want to format the coach concept a little bit differently. Feel free to change the following monologue to communicate your best ideas for using a coach.

"Your coach can be a youth leader, an adult sponsor, a teacher—any Christian adult you respect. Pick a coach that's the same gender as your team. Your coach doesn't actually join in your team meetings. He or she has a different job. His or her job is to hold you accountable to your regular meetings by asking you when you meet and how things are going. He or she advises you when there's a question, problem, or dispute in your team. And your coach prays for your team regularly. Remember, the coach doesn't actually meet with your team each week. Chances are, he or she has enough meetings to attend already!

   Okay, back to your Guidebooks. Take a moment to jot down some potential coaches for your team. Then circle the most likely candidate."

Again, give the students some time as they think through potential coaches and put them in their Guidebooks.

4. LIVE THE LIFE TOGETHER

START VIDEO [just over 10 minutes]
Shannon introduces the third step: LIVE THE LIFE TOGETHER. She shows us what a Life Together team might look like using the values we've already learned in the training this far.

Next is "Found Out, Part 5: All Together Now." Brad tells his friends what happened when he shared his faith with Leo.

Evangeline interrupts again and makes the point that we need to GET CONNECTED to share our faith with our friends.

Shannon wraps up for us. She helps the students understand how our lives would be different if we applied these principles to all of our relationships. "Get connected first with your team and then with everyone in your world."
STOP VIDEO

5. CONCLUSION

"The next step is yours. Are you willing to commit to a Life Together team outside of this training? Take the Gutsy Acts challenge on page 62 in your Guidebook."

Give students time to choose their Gutsy Acts.

C. Life Together small groups

"Okay, time for our Life Together groups here. All the principles we've talked about today apply to this group, too. Get into your groups and go through the questions on page 63."

Close in prayer.

Notes

Lesson Six
HAVE COURAGE

*I must **HAVE COURAGE** to do what I know Jesus wants me to do.*

Key Verse   John 16:33
Feelings   fearful, faithful
Facts   1. My fears are real, but my faith is stronger.
                   2. I can eliminate many of my fears through thoughtful planning.
                   3. The Holy Spirit is fearless, even when I'm not.

Actions
Now: I will identify my fears and build up my courage by examining my fears and working out a strategy that might overcome the worst of them.
This week: I will identify a courageous act to take in sharing my faith.
Long term: I will commit to a courageous act in sharing my faith and ask the Holy Spirit to work me over from the inside out.

In Short
You've learned a lot this week, you've taken many steps and made many commitments. But what will happen to all of this stuff when we're through with this training? Will you have the guts to carry on and carry out your intentions? This lesson will help you address and overcome the fears you may have about sharing your faith.

Background
In a sense, this lesson will have already been taught before it ever starts. Here's the lesson plan that preceded the lesson:

At the very beginning of the training, we asked students to check a list of fears in sharing the gospel in the Scared Silent section of their Guidebooks. Each subsequent lesson sent students back to the Scared Silent list to cross out any fears that were addressed and conquered in the previous lesson. Ideally, by now this list has been cut down to almost nothing. In addition, Gutsy Acts required students to make a commitment to carry out a courageous act in response to the lesson's message. By now students will have amassed a substantial list of courageous accomplishments.

So when Lesson Six finally comes around, they've spent time over the duration of this training identifying and overcoming fears and carrying out Gutsy Acts. In essence, Lesson Six merely asks students to share these courageous experiences, and then shows them how to do the same thing after the training is over.

Note: As part of this plan, the lesson itself can be entirely student led: the Student Presenters can host the extended Talkback and teach the key points that come out of it. The Youth Leader can wrap things up at the end.

Outline

A. Review **[5-7 minutes]**
   Flashback
B. The Point—HAVE COURAGE
   1. Intro: My Fear is Real; My Faith is Stronger **[8-10 minutes]**
   2. Scared (but not) Silent **[5-7 minutes]**
   3. Gutsy Acts **[5-7 minutes]**
   4. Conclusion **[7-9 minutes]**
C. Life Together small groups

A. Review

Welcome the group. Open in prayer.
   If you are using Student Presenters, explain that they will be doing most of the teaching in this lesson. We have written this lesson with Student Presenter cues for the majority of the monologues. If you are not using Student Presenters, you do the teaching at each of the Student Presenter's cues.

STUDENT PRESENTER:

"Guess what we are going to start with? Yep, what did we learn from last lesson? What stuck out the most?"

Allow students time to answer.

B. The Point—HAVE COURAGE

1. INTRO: MY FEAR IS REAL; MY FAITH IS STRONGER

START VIDEO [almost 6 minutes]
Shannon does a review of all five lessons and then introduces our last component of this training: HAVE COURAGE.
   We hear from The Professor in "It's Simple, Part 7: Courage!"
   Then Shannon takes us back to the Scared Silent survey.
STOP VIDEO

STUDENT PRESENTER:

Have students turn to the Scared Silent page in their Guidebooks.

"One of our greatest weapons against fear is to BE REAL with one another about our fears. Even after all the lessons, I'm still scared about sharing my faith *(share specific fear).*
   Look over your Scared Silent survey. Are there any fears you still have? You can bet that you're not the only one with that same fear. Anyone have the guts to be real with us about that fear or concern?"

After a fear has been expressed, ask if anyone has had that same fear but has managed to conquer it, and can offer some encouragement or advice. If no one offers advice, stop and pray for that person.

"These are real fears, and there's no way we can conquer every one of them! The good news is, we don't have to. We have someone who's bigger than us, who has conquered the world. Check out what Jesus has to say—"

Read John 16:33.

2. SCARED (BUT NOT) SILENT

START VIDEO [a little over 5 minutes]
First we see "Real Kids, Part 8: Scared But Not Silent."
   Then Shannon makes the point that "Faith is bigger than fear."
   Next is "Found Out, Part 6: The Day After." Brad talks with new Christian about what happened in the Lesson Four episode.
STOP VIDEO

3. GUTSY ACTS

STUDENT PRESENTER:
"In this training, we took part in another fear-buster called Gutsy Acts. _____ asked
Youth Leader
us to commit to one courageous action after each lesson and carry it out that day or week.
   For me, the toughest act was *(share personal story of the act and its result—why it was tough).* How about you?"

Interview students about their Gutsy Act stories: What was the act? What were your fears? How did you get past them? How do you feel about it now? Would you do it again? What would happen to your relationship with Jesus and others if you did this every day even after this training is over?

START VIDEO [just shy of 2 minutes]
Shannon and Evangeline explain that every act of faithful courage is a reminder of what we can do through Jesus; these memories strengthen us to share our faith.
STOP VIDEO

STUDENT PRESENTER:
"Earlier in the training, a few of you told us what it was like when you shared the gospel with someone. Let's see a few more snapshots. Anyone have the courage to tell us what happened when you shared your faith with a friend?"

Some follow-up questions as students share are: What was your worst fear before you did it? How did you overcome the fear? Were you scared while you did it? If you could offer encouragement to us when we're in that same situation, what would it be?

4. CONCLUSION

START VIDEO [exactly 4 minutes]
Here we see the final episode in the series, "Found Out, Part 7: The Last Person on Earth." Brad takes on the courageous act of SHARING THE GOSPEL with someone he never dreamed of sharing with before.
   Then Shannon wraps up the training for us.
STOP VIDEO

"We've got one more Gutsy Act to take. Turn to page 68 in your Guidebook. Work through the questions and choose your final Gutsy Act."

Allow students time to work through their Guidebooks. This Gutsy Act has a few more questions so it may take a little bit longer.

C. Life Together small groups

"Now it's time for our last Life Together group. Follow the discussion guide on page 69."

After the groups are finished, you can close your group however you think would be the most effective. We've written out a suggested closing, but tailor this time to your group's needs.

"Well, we're just about done with this training. Which seems like the right time to go to the very beginning. Here's the first thing I read to you: 2 Corinthians 3:18. Let's read it together."

Read the verse together. Then give a quick illustration of this verse as you saw it lived out by a student in the training.

Then pray for the students in the room, that they would live out the values taught throughout this training and have the courage to share their faith. Pray for friends outside of those in the training, that their hearts would be open to what they're about to hear; that the seed would take root, and that they would see Jesus reflected in the love of those in this room.

Notes

CREDITS

Live the Life Training

Training Director	Mike Work
Coordinator of Multimedia Ministries	June Dudley
Writer	Todd Temple
Concept Developer	Mark Oestreicher
Assistant to Director	Jennifer Tattersall
Editorial Assistant	Jodi Rhodes
Advisory Team	Bill Muir Geoff Cragg Byron Emmert Rich Van Pelt Lynn Ziegenfuss

Leader's Guide

Writers	Todd Temple Kaylyn Wilson
Editor	Sheri Stanley
Art Director	Deborah Razo/ Razdezignz

Student Guidebook

Editors	June Dudley Todd Temple Kaylyn Wilson
Art Director	Deborah Razo/ Razdezignz
Layout Artist	Oskar Ulloa
Contributing Writers	Neil Anderson Byron Emmert Jim Hancock Dan Marlow Josh McDowell Jenny Morgan Bill Muir Dave Park Dave Rahn Mike Work

Video

Writer/Producer	Todd Temple/ 10 TO 20
Directors	Blake Pilgreen Gary Hague/ Media Tech
Editor	Ryan Powell/ Media Tech
Graphics	Deborah Razo/ Razdezignz
Animation	Richard Brown/ Animal Productions

Additional video clips

Writer/Producer	Jim Hancock/ EdgeTV & IMS Productions (Real Kids, Found Out, It's Simple, What's a Christian? My House, Nadia's World, The Amazing Precision Marching Band)
Host	Shannon Lynch

Special thanks to:

Austin O'Brien	"Brad"
McNair Wilson	"Professor"
Larissa Kosits	"Evangeline"
Steve Bjorkman	Bridge Artist

Resources
from Youth Specialties

Professional Resources

Administration, Publicity, & Fundraising
  (Ideas Library)
Developing Student Leaders
Equipped to Serve:
  Volunteer Youth Worker Training Course
Help! I'm a Junior High Youth Worker!
Help! I'm a Small-Group Leader!
Help! I'm a Sunday School Teacher!
Help! I'm a Volunteer Youth Worker!
How to Expand Your Youth Ministry
How to Speak to Youth...and Keep Them Awake
  at the Same Time
Junior High Ministry (Updated & Expanded)
One Kid at a Time:
  Reaching Youth through Mentoring
Purpose-Driven Youth Ministry
So That's Why I Keep Doing This!
  52 Devotional Stories for Youth Workers
A Youth Ministry Crash Course
The Ministry of Nurture
The Youth Worker's Handbook to Family Ministry

Youth Ministry Programming

Camps, Retreats, Missions, & Service Ideas
  (Ideas Library)
Compassionate Kids: Practical Ways
  to Involve Your Students in Mission and Service
Creative Bible Lessons from the Old Testament
Creative Bible Lessons in John:
  Encounters with Jesus
Creative Bible Lessons in Romans: Faith on Fire!
Creative Bible Lessons on the Life of Christ
Creative Junior High Programs from A to Z,
  Vol. 1 (A-M)
Creative Junior High Programs from A to Z,
  Vol. 2 (N-Z)
Creative Meetings, Bible Lessons, & Worship
  Ideas (Ideas Library)
Crowd Breakers & Mixers (Ideas Library)
Drama, Skits, & Sketches (Ideas Library)
Dramatic Pauses
Facing Your Future: Graduating Youth Group
  with a Faith That Lasts
Games (Ideas Library)
Games 2 (Ideas Library)
Great Fundraising Ideas for Youth Groups
More Great Fundraising Ideas for Youth Groups
Great Retreats for Youth Groups
Greatest Skits on Earth
Greatest Skits on Earth, Vol. 2
Holiday Ideas (Ideas Library)
Hot Illustrations for Youth Talks
More Hot Illustrations for Youth Talks
Incredible Questionnaires for Youth Ministry
Junior High Game Nights
More Junior High Game Nights

Kickstarters: 101 Ingenious Intros to
  Just about Any Bible Lesson
Live the Life! Student Evangelism Training Kit
Memory Makers
Play It! Great Games for Groups
Play It Again! More Great Games for Groups
Special Events (Ideas Library)
Spontaneous Melodramas
Super Sketches for Youth Ministry
Teaching the Bible Creatively
What Would Jesus Do? Youth Leader's Kit
Wild Truth Bible Lessons
Wild Truth Bible Lessons 2
Worship Services for Youth Groups

Discussion Starters

Discussion & Lesson Starters (Ideas Library)
Discussion & Lesson Starters 2 (Ideas Library)
Get 'Em Talking
Keep 'Em Talking!
High School TalkSheets
More High School TalkSheets
High School TalkSheets: Psalms and Proverbs
Junior High TalkSheets
More Junior High TalkSheets
Junior High TalkSheets: Psalms and Proverbs
What If...? 450 Thought-Provoking Questions to Get
  Teenagers Talking, Laughing, and Thinking
Would You Rather...? 465 Provocative Questions to
  Get Teenagers Talking
Have You Ever...? 450 Intriguing Questions Guaran-
  teed to Get Teenagers Talking

Clip Art

ArtSource Vols. 1-7 on CD-ROM
ArtSource Vol. 8–Stark Raving Clip Art

Videos

EdgeTV
The Heart of Youth Ministry: A Morning
  with Mike Yaconelli
Next Time I Fall in Love Video Curriculum
Real Kids, Real Life, Real Faith–Video
  Discussion-Starting Series
Understanding Your Teenager Video Curriculum

Student Books

Grow For It Journal
Grow For It Journal through the Scriptures
What Would Jesus Do? Spiritual Challenge Journal
Wild Truth Journal for Junior Highers